Rise Up, Shepherd!

Rise Up, Shepherd!

Advent Reflections on the Spirituals

LUKE A. POWERY

WESTMINSTER
JOHN KNOX PRESS
LOUISVILLE · KENTUCKY

First edition
Published by Westminster John Knox Press
Louisville, Kentucky

17 18 19 20 21 22 23 24 25 26—10 9 8 7 6 5 4 3 2 1

Book design by Sharon Adams
Cover design by designpointinc.com
Cover illustration: Blessings, *1992 (oil on canvas)* © *by Bernard Stanley Hoyes /*
Private Collection / Bridgeman Images

Library of Congress Cataloging-in-Publication Data

Names: Powery, Luke A., 1974– author.
Title: Rise up, shepherd! : Advent reflections on the spirituals / Luke A. Powery.
Description: First edition. | Louisville, KY : Westminster John Knox Press, 2017.
Identifiers: LCCN 2017013695 (print) | LCCN 2017027428 (ebook) | ISBN 9781611648287 (ebk.) | ISBN 9780664260323 (pbk. : alk. paper)
Subjects: LCSH: Advent—Meditations. | Spirituals (Songs)—Meditations.
Classification: LCC BV40 (ebook) | LCC BV40 .P69 2017 (print) | DDC 242/.332—dc23
LC record available at https://lccn.loc.gov/2017013695

Most Westminster John Knox Press books are available at special quantity discounts when purchased in bulk by corporations, organizations, and special-interest groups. For more information, please e-mail SpecialSales@wjkbooks.com.

For Sam Hammond

Contents

Week Three

Week Four

Preface

We live in a fractured world. Read the newspapers or an Internet story or the latest blog, and it is easy to see how divided society is—politically, racially, economically, and religiously. These societal splinters can create a sense of hopelessness and despair with no end in sight. This is where the Spirituals come in, those songs sung by weary throats, created in a brutal historical setting of slavery by the enslaved, yet resonating with hope through all the sinister splinters of social sin. They are musical memorabilia of hope in seemingly helpless situations. These songs, these musical lifelines, reveal the possibility of hope in hellish circumstances, light in the midst of darkness, love in the face of hate. When brutally treated in slavery, the enslaved, the unknown black bards, still sang out, "there's room for many a mo'!" It is this future present hope embedded in the Spirituals that led me to put them into conversation with the historic Christian liturgical season of Advent, a season that is itself built on the hope of the coming of Jesus Christ.

Bringing the Spirituals and Advent together is a way to pray for a double blessing of hope. Like with an espresso, sometimes one shot is not enough; you need a double or triple shot to lift you from the malaise of the day. In similar fashion, these brief daily meditations on the Spirituals for the season of Advent are a double shot to lift our spirits that might be low due to the tension in the world. Joining the message of the Spirituals with the overall narrative and movement of Advent is also a way to bridge worlds that do not normally converge—a cultural musical literature of faith born in slavery and pervasive in the Black Church and a high liturgical sensibility of the church calendar, in this case, Advent. This book bridges my own background in music and the Church with the rich and meaningful liturgical tradition of my current pastoral call, Duke University Chapel. This intermingling of cultures and traditions is a sign of the Spirit and unveils that the divisiveness of the day need not be the way forward. The twain can meet.

Just as the Spirituals, songs of the Spirit, traversed cultures for many years, initially out of the bowels of enslavement to the concert halls of Europe, and continue to be sung all throughout the world in different settings and languages, this book attempts a similar boundary-crossing of past, present, and future, with the aim of instilling Advent hope in the readers. Of course, the aim is to nourish spiritually those who encounter the words on these pages through Advent reflections on the historical cultural literature of the Spirituals. But the subtext of this main text is to remember the future God has for us—a blending of time, culture, tradition, race, gender, and class into a beautiful bouquet of unity where all walls of division vanish. This daily devotional has an eternal gaze toward the reconciliation of all things, the bringing together of difference in the unity of the Holy Spirit.

The Spirituals as expressions of the Spirit are perfect for bridging the worlds of the past, present, and future through the season of Advent. The method is simple. Every day of Advent will have a Spiritual chosen as the main text for reflection, nodding to a historical understanding of them as a "Third Testament." Options of canonical Scripture readings are offered for each day with a portion of one included after the reflection on the Spiritual of the day. Each day closes with a short prayer that can also be used. The hope is that you will discover hope afresh through these words. Priority is given to the Spirituals, the voices of the enslaved, the unlettered, the forgotten, the illiterate, as a way to learn from those whose voices are not often heard in society, church, or academy. Thus, it is critical to learn from these marginalized voices in a liturgical season where hope is found in a humble baby Jesus born in poverty. My approach is an implicit call to remember that hope may be found on the edges of society.

These daily reflections will help us to remember the Spirituals and Advent, and the worlds they represent, together. This talk about remembering and memory would be much thinner if I did not remember those who nudged this project forward. Many educational institutions and conferences stoked the fire of the Spirituals in my bones through their generous invitations to present; the comments, questions, and overall feedback from these various sessions showed me how relevant the Spirituals are for today and not just yesterday. Also, early on in my tenure at Duke, Sam Hammond, "the living legend," Duke University's carillonneur for over 50 years, sat in my office to discuss the Spirituals and one of my other books. It was in that conversation that Sam, unbeknown to him, confirmed the deep sense I had prior to coming to Duke, by suggesting that I write some daily meditations on the Spirituals for the liturgical year. He encouraged such a project as this and encouraged me; thus I dedicate this book to Sam, a man who rings bells in the Spirit at Duke Chapel every day. Sam is a part of the Duke Chapel staff and community. This spiritual community has been my home for the last five years, and it is one immersed in the liturgical year and thus in the pattern of Christ, upon which the church calendar is based. These brothers and sisters from diverse walks of life have given me a deeper appreciation for the liturgical calendar, which is why I focus on Advent. In addition, Duke Divinity School has also encouraged teaching on the Spirituals, which only keeps the fire burning for these songs! Furthermore, I cannot forget my brothers and sisters from the African diaspora in the church and academy who nurture my love for the Spirituals, the Spirit's song, through performance and study.

Since this project is not created in a vacuum but among a cloud of witnesses, past and present, I have to remember Tim Buskey, my extraordinary research assistant, who worked tirelessly on organizing this book in its early stage; he was meticulous and always curious and without him, this book may have never made it to the publisher's desk. Of course, there would be no published work without a publisher, and Westminster John Knox graciously jumped on board for this project, ushered into their system by the wise hands of executive editor Robert Ratcliff, to whom I am grateful for his ongoing cheerleading throughout the years. Intellectual communities, spiritual communities, cultural communities, research assistants, editors, and publishers are key to making a book come to fruition, but even more so, in my case, is the family unit of my dear wife, Gail, and my precious children, Moriah and Zachary, who sustain me. I can speak about and sing the Spirituals because they make me sing and blow sweet music into my life. Without them, without God, none of this is possible.

Divisions will not cease without the intervention of God. That being said, dear reader, I leave you with a prayer: May the words of my mouth on the written page and the meditations of all of our hearts be acceptable in the sight of God, who is our Rock and Redeemer. May these daily words for Advent become the Word of God for you and fan the flames of hope, filling your hearts with anticipation for the coming of God into the world. The early church said, "Come, Lord Jesus" (Rev. 22). This book, along with the Spirituals, says the same thing in another way: "Rise up, shepherd."

Luke A. Powery

Week One

Day 1

Psalm 25:1–10; Nehemiah 9:6–15; 1 Thessalonians 5:1–11

Ain't Dat Good News?

Got a crown up in de Kingdom, ain't dat good news?
Got a crown up in de Kingdom, ain't dat good news?

Refrain
I'm a goin' to lay down dis world,
Goin' to shoulder up mah cross,
Goin' to take it home to Jesus, ain't dat good news?

Got a harp up in de Kingdom, ain't dat good news?
Got a harp up in de Kingdom, ain't dat good news?
Refrain

Got a robe up in de Kingdom, ain't dat good news?
Got a robe up in de Kingdom, ain't dat good news?
Refrain

Got a slippers in de Kingdom, ain't dat good news?
Got a slippers in de Kingdom, ain't dat good news?
Refrain

Got a Savior in de Kingdom, ain't dat good news?
Got a Savior in de Kingdom, ain't dat good news?
Refrain

—*Songs of Zion*, 114*

As we yearn for the future kingdom of God and gaze toward the other world, it is true that our hope for "de Kingdom" doesn't relieve us from "mah cross." The images of future crowns, harps, robes, and slippers provided good news, especially for those who didn't have the economic privilege to purchase crowns, harps, robes, or slippers. Those who had no shoes could rejoice in the heavenly slippers that were to come. Most of all, that a Savior was in the kingdom was good news. Moreover, the cross one carried could be given over to Jesus in the end as eternal relief, bringing joy and a sense of gladness, even if the world's situation was currently burdensome. To know that what one did not have in this world would be provided in the next gave hope in the present.

One doesn't want to be so otherworldly that he is no earthly good, but it's clear that, despite our shrinking from emphasizing a future home with "mah Jesus," there is a home prepared for us. This eternal home is our ultimate destiny. Good news is our end. Today may not be full of good news but we are marching toward it, and what we lack today will be given to us tomorrow. This is good news. Crowns as children of God. Harps to express the joy of our hearts. Robes to be clothed in light and righteousness. Slippers to walk all around the kingdom. A Savior to save us from ourselves and our pain. No more crosses to bear, just joys to share. Ain't dat good news? It is great news. Rejoice today.

Songs of Zion (Nashville: Abingdon Press, 1981), 114.

For God has destined us not for wrath but for obtaining salvation through our Lord Jesus Christ, who died for us, so that whether we are awake or asleep we may live with him.

(1 Thess. 5:9–10)

Prayer for the Day
Good news God, thank you for a kingdom where we can lay down our crosses and find eternal rest.

Day 2

Psalm 25:1–10; Nehemiah 9:16–25;
1 Thessalonians 5:12–22

'Tis the Old Ship of Zion

Refrain
'Tis the old ship of Zion,
'Tis the old ship of Zion,
'Tis the old ship of Zion, Git on board, Git on board.

It has landed many a thousand,
It has landed many a thousand,
It has landed many a thousand,
Git on board, Git on board.

Ain't no danger in de water,
Ain't no danger in de water,
Ain't no danger in de water,
Git on board, Git on board.

It was good for my dear mother, . . .

It was good for my dear father, . . .

It will take you home to Glory, . . .

—Songs of Zion, 131

Water can be refreshing. A cool drink on a hot day. A reviving swim in a pool when wearied after a long day's work. Moisture for plant soil after several dry days of the hot sun. Yet water can also be dangerous. Children drown in pools or in the ocean. Shark attacks take place near the beach shores during hot summer days. Celebrities have been found dead in bathtub water.

Waters can be treacherous from storms or, with those enslaved in mind, it is known that during the Middle Passage, many were thrown overboard from slave ships and left to drown in the seas. Water became a natural grave. No wonder we are told "ain't no danger in de water." To know there is safe passage in waters that have been detrimental is an encouragement.

Also, it is "the old ship of Zion" that will carry one safely. It is God who is faithful to lead the way and transport us to the other side, to home. And we know this isn't the first time God has done this. It has been done for the thousands, including our mothers and fathers. That cloud of witnesses calls to us across the waters, beckoning us to take the risk with God. Will you git on board and trust God, knowing that God has a history of helping? Ain't no danger on God's ship.

[Y]ou in your great mercies did not forsake them in the wilderness; the pillar of cloud that led them in the way did not leave them by day, nor the pillar of fire by night that gave them light on the way by which they should go. You gave your good spirit to instruct them, and did not withhold your manna from their mouths, and gave them water for their thirst. For forty years you sustained them in the wilderness so that they lacked nothing; their clothes did not wear out and their feet did not swell.

(Neh. 9:19–21)

Prayer for the Day
Faithful God, though the seas can be sinister, help us to realize that your ship will keep us safe.

Day 3

Psalm 25:1–10; Nehemiah 9:26–31; Luke 21:20–24

Come Out de Wilderness

Tell me, how did you feel when you
come out de wilderness,
come out de wilderness,
come out de wilderness?
How did you feel when you
come out de wilderness?
Leaning on de Lord,

Refrain
I'm a leaning on de Lord,
I'm a leaning on de Lord,
I'm a leaning on de Lord,
Who died on Calvary.

Well, I loved ev'rybody when I
come out de wilderness,
come out de wilderness,
come out de wilderness?

> Loved ev'rybody when I
> come out de wilderness?
> Leaning on de Lord,
> *Refrain*
>
> Well, my soul was so happy when I
> come out de wilderness,
> come out de wilderness,
> come out de wilderness?
> Soul was so happy when I
> come out de wilderness?
> Leaning on de Lord,
> *Refrain*
>
> —*Songs of Zion*, 136

The spiritual for today emphasizes "come out de wilderness." It is the linguistic motif that overshadows even "leaning on de Lord." Why might that be? First, it is the recognition that the wilderness is a common human experience. It is a part of the Christian journey and unavoidable. That one word—wilderness—echoes in the ears of any singer. The wilderness is a wild place with no water, no food, seemingly unaccompanied by anyone or anything. It is a trying place, a dry desert for a parched people. Second, we see the affirmation that not only is the wilderness a reality but that we will "come out" of it. This is a promise—that trouble "don't last always" and neither do wildernesses. Trouble is for a time perhaps, but not for eternity. We will "come out."

And God will provide the way out of the wilderness for we have been "leaning on de Lord." The refrain stresses this and each verse ends with this phrase to remind us that no one comes out of the wilderness without God, without leaning on the everlasting arms of the Lord. We can't "come out" without help. But if we lean, we will learn how we've been changed through the wilderness experience.

The third suggestion in this spiritual is that we will come out of the wilderness as different people. How else could we love everybody when we come out? We are happy because of the freedom from the wilderness. There's great relief from coming out, but this will only occur if we lean on God. Just as each verse closes with that notion, may we always end up doing the same thing: "leaning on de Lord."

> Make me to know your ways, O Lord; teach me your paths. Lead me in your truth, and teach me, for you are the God of my salvation; for you I wait all day long.
>
> (Ps. 25:4–5)

Prayer for the Day
Though I endure a wilderness, help me, O God, to realize that I can lean on you for deliverance because you will lead me out of the wilderness to a path of happiness.

Day 4

Jeremiah 33:14–16; Psalm 25:1–10;
Luke 21:25–36; 1 Thessalonians 3:9–13

Hold Out to the End

All dem Mount Zion member, dey have many ups and
  downs;
But cross come or no come, for to hold out to the end.

Hold out to the end, hold out to the end.
It is my 'termination for to hold out to the end.
          —*Slave Songs of the United States* (1867), 76[*]

As we celebrate this Advent season, remembering the coming of Christ to the world, his first coming and eventual
second coming, it is true that perseverance and patience
are necessary. From the days of my youth, and maybe
yours, I've heard "soon and very soon" but "soon" seems
to be taking a while, a long while. While we wait for the
coming of the Son of Man, we can't live in the clouds of

---

[*]William Francis Allen, Charles Pickard Ware, and Lucy Mckim Gar-
rison, eds., *Slave Songs of the United States* (New York: A. Simpson and
Co., 1867).

glory; we live through life on earth with its "many ups and downs." All people of God, or as this spiritual says, "All dem Mount Zion member," have highs and lows in life. This is human existence on earth.

But what sets the people of God apart is their "'termination for to hold out to the end." There is an embedded hope in us that propels us forward to hold out to the end, believing that redemption is near. This dogged faith is what is required when we wait with seemingly no end in sight, a faith that will last till the end. The end is with God, so waiting and holding out is worth it. Ups and downs occur, but in the end God will be there. It will be worth the wait.

> There will be signs in the sun, the moon, and the stars, and on the earth distress among nations confused by the roaring of the sea and the waves. People will faint from fear and foreboding of what is coming upon the world, for the powers of the heavens will be shaken. Then they will see "the Son of Man coming in a cloud" with power and great glory. Now when these things begin to take place, stand up and raise your heads, because your redemption is drawing near.
>
> (Luke 21:25–28)

Prayer for the Day
Through my ups and downs, help me to never give up and never lose hope that You, O God, are my beginning and my end. Let the hope of tomorrow reshape my today.

Day 5

Numbers 17:1–11; Psalm 90; 2 Peter 3:1–18

Swing Low, Sweet Chariot

Refrain
Swing low, sweet chariot,
Coming for to carry me home:
Swing low, sweet chariot,
Coming for to carry me home.

I looked over Jordan, and what did I see,
Coming for to carry me home?
A band of angels coming after me,
Coming for to carry me home.
Refrain

If you get there before I do,
Coming for to carry me home;
Tell all my friends I'm coming too,
Coming for to carry me home.
Refrain

I'm sometimes up, I'm sometimes down,
Coming for to carry me home;

But still my soul feels heavenly bound,
Coming for to carry me home.
Refrain

—*Songs of Zion*, 104

This classic, well-known spiritual is a favorite for many people across the world. It paints the picture of going home, of being heavenly bound. There's joy in this song, a deep yearning and hope to be carried home. "Home" is popular in many spirituals as the enslaved were separated from their native homes, thus their families and friends and cultures. Home is where one is known and loved. Home can be the epitome of community. It is a place of refuge and safety. This is why the old saying is true: "There's no place like home." You can't escape "home," as it is repeated over and over again in this spiritual; and on the call-and-response verses, "coming for to carry me home" is sung by the whole community, bringing greater emphasis to this hope.

The hope for home includes the notion that we can't get there by our own power. We can't reach the other side of Jordan with being clever or networked. There is a deep belief that we will be carried home by this sweet chariot. We need help to make it home, finally. In the meantime, we keep moving toward the end, not knowing when the chariot will swing low to pick us up for the eternal ride. We keep moving, just as this spiritual was not only about going to heaven but going to freedom on earth, even reaching the North to be out of slavery. Home is where we will be free. God wants us to be free. God want us to find our home in him, the One who is our refuge and strength, our strong tower. Come home, not to your neighborhood, but to the abiding, loving presence of God.

But do not ignore this one fact, beloved, that with the Lord one day is like a thousand years, and a thousand years are like one day. The Lord is not slow about his promise, as some think of slowness, but is patient with you, not wanting any to perish, but all to come to repentance. But the day of the Lord will come like a thief, and then the heavens will pass away with a loud noise, and the elements will be dissolved with fire, and the earth and everything that is done on it will be disclosed.

(2 Pet. 3:8–10)

Prayer for the Day

Dear Lord, carry me home to your presence in the midst of today's ups and downs. Swing by and touch me with the hope of our eternal home.

Day 6

2 Samuel 7:18–29; Psalm 90; Revelation 22:12–16

Good News, the Chariot's Coming

Refrain
Good news, the chariot's coming,
Good news, the chariot's coming,
Good news, the chariot's coming,
And I don't want-her to leave-a-me behind.

It's a golden chariot,—Carry me home,
A golden chariot,—Carry me home,
A golden chariot,—Carry me home,
And I don't want-her to leave-a-me behind.
Refrain

There's a long white robe, In the heaven I know;
A long white robe,—In the heaven I know;
A long white robe,—In the heaven I know;

And I don't want-her to leave-a-me behind.
Refrain

—*Folk Song of the American
Negro* (1915), 49[*]

If we gaze out on the landscape of current events, it would be easy to see lots of bad news—violence, hatred, poverty, discrimination, civil wars—the list seems to be eternal. Tragedy is so prevalent it appears to be a comedy, a laughingstock of our human plight, laughing to keep from crying. Pain is perpetual in our day, even if we consider the physical ailments of others. This raw truth is everywhere in the spirituals. Melancholic misery resonates through these songs.

At the same time, hope is born through them. Hope, both otherworldly and this-worldly, is present. Amid brutal degradation, the human imagination peers into eternity and sees long white robes and golden chariots. It envisions a better day, another day, another world, God's world. There's a faithful recognition that all we see is not all there is. Empirical studies can't erase eternal realities. There is "good news" in this upbeat spiritual. Good news that a chariot is coming, or as Jesus says, "I am coming soon." There's so much active love from God that God chooses to come to us, even without our permission or volition. The chariot's coming. God is coming. Coming to you to carry you. This is good news, indeed. Receive the good news because I don't want you to be left behind.

---

[*]John Wesley Work (ed.), *Folk Song of the American Negro* (Nashville: Press of Fisk University, 1915).

"See, I am coming soon; my reward is with me, to repay according to everyone's work. I am the Alpha and the Omega, the first and the last, the beginning and the end."

(Rev. 22:12–13)

Prayer for the Day

When no one else cares, when no one else sees, you see my need and you come to carry me. Come and allow me to experience the joy and good news of your presence.

Day 7

Psalm 90; Isaiah 1:24–31; Luke 11:29–32

I've Been 'Buked

I've been 'buked an' I've been scorned,
I've been 'buked an' I've been scorned, children.
I've been 'buked an' I've been scorned,
I've been talked about sho's you' born.

Dere is trouble all over dis worl',
Dere is trouble all over dis worl', children.
Dere is trouble all over dis worl',
Dere is trouble all over dis worl'.

Ain' gwine lay my 'ligion down,
Ain' gwine lay my 'ligion down, children.
Ain' gwine lay my 'ligion down,
Ain' gwine lay my 'ligion down.

—*Songs of Zion*, 143

The Christian journey is not all roses. There are also thorns. There are times when you might say, "I've been 'buked an' I've been scorned." Maybe you've been the topic of conversations for ill purposes or you've endured broken relations. Beyond your own personal orbit, the world is just as bad. You can't miss that fact as we hear repeated: "Dere is trouble all over dis worl'." Advent isn't just a time of the coming of God. It is a time of judgment, something not discussed often in the church, a time of searching and penitence. Grace is so much more popular, yet there's a time when scorning happens and trouble terrorizes. How do you respond when grace seems to have taken a vacation?

Advent is also a season of waiting. It takes patience, even through tough times. But the question remains whether you will respond like this spiritual, "Ain' gwine lay my 'ligion down," translated, "I'm not going to lay my religion down." I'm not going to lay aside my faith. I may not understand everything that is happening in my life. I may be enduring a rough path in life right now but I am determined not to lay aside my religion, my faith, God. The decision to not lay aside one's faith is really an acknowledgment that God didn't bring you this far to leave you, that God has been faithful on your journey, that you can count on God because God has proven that God cares. The storms may come, the winds may blow, tornadoes may spin, but let this be the day of determination in your life to refuse to give in to the troubles of the world and assert "Ain' gwine lay my 'ligion down." Why would you? God has never laid you down but laid his own life down in Christ for you.

> Zion shall be redeemed by justice,
>   and those in her who repent, by righteousness.
> But rebels and sinners shall be destroyed together,
>   and those who forsake the LORD shall be
>   consumed.

For you shall be ashamed of the oaks
    in which you delighted;
and you shall blush for the gardens
    that you have chosen.
For you shall be like an oak
    whose leaf withers,
      and like a garden without water.
The strong shall become like tinder,
    and their work like a spark;
they and their work shall burn together,
    with no one to quench them.
                    (Isa. 1:27–31)

Prayer for the Day
Faithful God, you never laid me aside. Give me the courage and strength to never lay you or my faith down because you are the one who lifts me up.

Week Two

Day 1

Malachi 3:5–12; Luke 1:68–79; Philippians 1:12–18a

I Want to Be Ready

Refrain
I want to be ready, I want to be ready,
I want to be ready to walk in Jerusalem just like John.

O John, O John, what do you say?
Walk in Jerusalem just like John.
That I'll be there at the coming day,
Walk in Jerusalem just like John.
Refrain

John said the city was just four-square
Walk in Jerusalem just like John.
And he declared he'd meet me there,
Walk in Jerusalem just like John.
Refrain

When Peter was preaching at Pentecost,
Walk in Jerusalem just like John.
He was endowed with the Holy Ghost,

Walk in Jerusalem just like John.
Refrain
                    —*Songs of Zion*, 151

We should prepare for Advent. If we know a guest is coming to our home, we prepare the place and get it in order. Of course, there can always be surprise visits, some of them being unwelcomed, catching us off guard, unprepared. But every year we have Advent. Every year, we anticipate the coming of God in Christ to the world. Every year, we have the opportunity to get ready. This spiritual implies that a certain kind of readiness is needed to "walk in Jerusalem." This Jerusalem is the new Jerusalem, a new heaven and new earth, where the inhabitants are people like John, the revelator, and Peter, both saints of old. These saints have shown the walkway to this land and they are waiting to "meet [us] there." Thus, this isn't a lonely journey. Others are preparing with us to take the walk of a lifetime, and others have blazed the trail ahead of us and are cheering us on in that great cloud of witnesses.

I want to be ready and get ready. How about you?

> "And you, child, will be called the prophet of the
>   Most High;
>   for you will go before the Lord to prepare his ways,
> to give knowledge of salvation to his people
>   by the forgiveness of their sins.
> By the tender mercy of our God,
>   the dawn from on high will break upon us,
> to give light to those who sit in darkness and in the
>   shadow of death,
>   to guide our feet into the way of peace."
>   (Luke 1:76–79)

Prayer for the Day

Guide my feet while I run this race. Prepare me to walk into your arms on that great coming day and shine your Spirit on my path to illumine the walkway to Jerusalem. I want to be ready. Help me be ready.

Day 2

Malachi 3:13–18; Luke 1:68–79; Philippians 1:18b–26

Standin' in the Need of Prayer

Not my brother, nor my sister, but it's me, O Lord,
Standin' in the need of prayer;
Not my brother, nor my sister, but it's me, O Lord,
Standin' in the need of prayer.

Refrain
It's me, it's me, it's me, O Lord,
Standin' in the need of prayer;
It's me, it's me, it's me, O Lord,
Standin' in the need of prayer;

Not the preacher, nor the deacon, but it's me, O Lord,
Standin' in the need of prayer;
Not the preacher, nor the deacon, but it's me, O Lord,
Standin' in the need of prayer.
Refrain

Not my father, nor my mother, but it's me, O Lord,
Standin' in the need of prayer;

Not my father, nor my mother, but it's me, O Lord,
Standin' in the need of prayer.
Refrain

Not the stranger, nor my neighbor, but it's me, O Lord,
Standin' in the need of prayer;
Not the stranger, nor my neighbor, but it's me, O Lord,
Standin' in the need of prayer.
Refrain

—*Songs of Zion*, 110

"It's me . . . standin' in the need of prayer." We may
not want to admit it but we are always in need of prayer.
We may want to believe that someone else needs prayer
before us—our brothers, sisters, fathers, mothers, preach-
ers, deacons, strangers, or neighbors—but if we are hon-
est, which is what I love about this spiritual, *we* are in
need of prayer. Survey your life and canvass the neighborhood of your heart, and see what your need is. Name
it before God unashamedly. Perhaps you've been pouring
out your life for others, and this is good, in and of itself,
but not if you neglect yourself. You have needs also, and
there's nothing wrong about standing before God in your
prayer closet and whispering today, "Lord, it's me. I'm
the one in need. I come just as I am, in need of prayer. I'm
so desperate and tired but I'm standing. I'm weak at the
knees but I'm standing. I'm standing to get your atten-
tion. Hear my cry, O Lord."

This is not selfish spirituality but saving spirituality
because prayer is a form of love—love for others and
love for the self—and we are called to love our neighbors as ourselves. But if we don't love ourselves enough to
pray for ourselves, we don't have enough love to extend
to another. Make your requests known to God with

confidence that God will hear and answer your prayer because God sees and knows your need. Why wouldn't this be true when God is Emmanuel, a God with us at every point of life?

> Yes, and I will continue to rejoice, for I know that through your prayers and the help of the Spirit of Jesus Christ this will result in my deliverance. It is my eager expectation and hope that I will not be put to shame in any way, but that by my speaking with all boldness, Christ will be exalted now as always in my body, whether by life or by death. For to me, living is Christ and dying is gain.
>
> (Phil. 1:18c–21)

Prayer for the Day

Seeing God, I'm standing in need of prayer. You knew that before I even said it. Answer when I call. You know who it is. It's me, your child. It's me, the one you love.

Day 3

Malachi 4:1–6; Luke 1:68–79; Luke 9:1–6

Free at Last

Free at last, free at last,
Thank God a'mighty I'm free at last.

Surely been 'buked, and surely been scorned,
Thank God a'mighty, I'm free at last.
But still my soul is-a heaven born,
Thank God a'mighty, I'm free at last.

If you don't know that I been redeemed,
Thank God a'mighty, I'm free at last.
Just follow me down to Jordan's stream,
Thank God a'mighty, I'm free at last.
—*Songs of Zion*, 80

The United States prides itself on being a free democratic society. Often citizens praise the civic and religious freedoms they have in this country. Yet someone else's freedom may enslave another. Historically, we've seen this in the Americas, which is the historical context of "Free

31

at Last." Enslaved humans were bound, but a time came when they were delivered and thanked God Almighty they were "free at last." Freedom didn't come quickly. Some didn't make it to earthly freedom but only a heavenly freedom. Regardless, they thanked God because God was the deliverer.

From what do you need to be set free? What has you bound? God wants you free. Though you "been 'buked and scorned," though there has been trouble on every hand in your life, freedom is coming. Even as freedom comes, know that when one is free, one is not just free *from* something but free *for* something. You will be free, but for what? That's the next step.

> But for you who revere my name the sun of righteousness shall rise, with healing in its wings. You shall go out leaping like calves from the stall. And you shall tread down the wicked, for they will be ashes under the soles of your feet, on the day when I act, says the LORD of hosts.
>
> (Mal. 4:2–3)

Prayer for the Day
Delivering God, free me to be all that you want me to be.

Day 4

Malachi 3:1–4; Luke 1:68–79;
Luke 3:1–6; Philippians 1:3–11

Go, Tell It on the Mountain

Refrain
Go, tell it on the mountain,
Over the hills and everywhere,
Go, tell it on the mountain
That Jesus Christ is born.

While shepherds kept their watching
O'er silent flocks by night,
Behold throughout the heavens
There shone a holy light.
Refrain

The shepherds feared and trembled
When lo! above the earth
Rang out the angel chorus
That hailed our Savior's birth.
Refrain

Down in a lowly manger
The humble Christ was born,

And God sent us salvation
That blessed Christmas morn.
Refrain

—*Songs of Zion*, 75

"Advent" means "coming." In particular, it refers to the first coming of Jesus Christ into the world in a lowly manger and the second coming of Christ, who will return as reigning King to redeem all of creation. In this well-known spiritual, there is a declaration of what we should do in response to the news that Jesus Christ is born. "Go, tell." It reminds us that both in word and deed, we are called to respond to the Savior's birth, his humble coming into the world. It is a charge to act, to move, and to speak. In other words, can I get a witness? Are we witnesses to the living Christ who came on "Christmas morn"?

The creator of this spiritual does not suggest we keep quiet and keep this news to ourselves. The music of this song is upbeat and bouncing with joy, and this call, this charge, should be good news to us. The "go, tell" is an invitation to experience the joy of Jesus and spread this joy wherever we may find ourselves. It's the combination that is key. We can go somewhere and never say one word. Or we can speak but never go. Witnessing to the birth of Jesus requires both—going and telling, acting and speaking—because Jesus requires our whole being, not just one part but our bodies and voices, the fullness of who we are. Let his coming come to you in such a way today that you can't help but be filled with the energy to go and tell some good news in a world full of bad news.

[John] went into all the region around the Jordan, proclaiming a baptism of repentance for the forgiveness of sins, as it is written in the book of the words of the prophet Isaiah,

> "The voice of one crying out in the wilderness:
> 'Prepare the way of the Lord,
>   make his paths straight.
> Every valley shall be filled,
> and every mountain and hill shall be made low,
> and the crooked shall be made straight,
> and the rough ways made smooth;
> and all flesh shall see the salvation of God.'"
>
> (Luke 3:3–6)

Prayer for the Day

Coming God, come into my life that I may receive the joy of going and telling the good news of your birth in the world.

Day 5

Psalm 126; Isaiah 40:1–11; Romans 8:22–25

Bye and Bye

Refrain
O bye and bye, bye and bye,
O bye and bye, yes, bye and bye
I'm goin' to lay down dis heavy load.

I know my robe's goin' to fit me well.
I'm goin' to lay down dis heavy load;
O I tried it on at the gates of hell.
I'm goin' to lay down dis heavy load.
Refrain

Hell is deep and dark despair,
I'm goin' to lay down dis heavy load;
Stop, po' sinner, and don't go there,
I'm goin' to lay down dis heavy load.
Refrain

O Christians, can't you rise and tell,
I'm goin' to lay down dis heavy load;

That Jesus hath done all things well,
I'm goin' to lay down dis heavy load.
Refrain

—*Songs of Zion*, 164

There are some things to which we should say "bye," "so long," "see you later." There are things that we endure that will not last forever. The sufferings of this present time won't determine our future, nor will we carry it to the end. "Dis heavy load," whatever it might be, will be laid down, eventually. What is your heavy load that you want to lay down: a psychological, emotional, financial, relational, or social burden? Are you determined to lay it down? Can you say, "I'm goin' to lay down dis heavy load"? Perhaps you didn't even notice that you were weighted down by "dis heavy load."

But what is certain is that the impetus of laying the load down is "that Jesus hath done all things well." "I'm going to do something," but Jesus is active too. He does things and does them well. He is the burden bearer and declares, "Come to me, all you that are weary and are carrying heavy burdens, and I will give you rest" (Matt. 11:28). Cast your cares on him. Put down your load and pick up your rest.

We know that the whole creation has been groaning in labor pains until now; and not only the creation, but we ourselves, who have the first fruits of the Spirit, groan inwardly while we wait for adoption, the redemption of our bodies. For in hope we were saved. Now hope that is seen is not hope. For who hopes for what is seen? But if we hope for what we do not see, we wait for it with patience.

(Rom. 8:22–25)

Prayer for the Day
God of hope, today I groan but help me to learn that my groaning is going somewhere—toward redemption found in You. Set me free to hope even while I groan.

Day 6

Psalm 126; Isaiah 19:18–25; 2 Peter 1:2–15

I'm Gonna Sing

I'm gonna sing when the Spirit says a-sing,
I'm gonna sing when the Spirit says a-sing,
I'm gonna sing when the Spirit says a-sing,
And obey the Spirit of the Lord.

I'm gonna shout when the Spirit says a-shout,
I'm gonna shout when the Spirit says a-shout,
I'm gonna shout when the Spirit says a-shout,
And obey the Spirit of the Lord.

I'm gonna preach when the Spirit says a-preach,
I'm gonna preach when the Spirit says a-preach,
I'm gonna preach when the Spirit says a-preach,
And obey the Spirit of the Lord.

I'm gonna pray when the Spirit says a-pray,
I'm gonna pray when the Spirit says a-pray,
I'm gonna pray when the Spirit says a-pray,
And obey the Spirit of the Lord.

I'm gonna sing when the Spirit says a-sing,
I'm gonna sing when the Spirit says a-sing,
I'm gonna sing when the Spirit says a-sing,
And obey the Spirit of the Lord.

—*Songs of Zion*, 81

The Spirit is a wind of God that blows where it wills (John 3). In light of this, it's not easy to follow or listen to the Spirit. How does one obey the Wind? Repeatedly, the spiritual singer speaks of obeying the Spirit of the Lord. This seems to be the aim or hope, no matter if it is singing, shouting, preaching, or praying. The key is to act "when the Spirit says." The Spirit moves in mysterious ways and may not shout in your ear but whisper in your heart. How do we discern the movement of the Spirit? That is the question, even though the spiritual seems so assured of knowing the speech of the Spirit. But it is this confidence, this spiritual courage, that calls us to a way of being that we may not be used to embodying. It calls us, challenges us, to obey and to know what the Spirit says. It calls us to learn the speech of God, which we can discern in life in order to act, rather than disobey and have our own way. It calls us to pray for such discernment and a desire to not act, unless the Spirit tells us to do so. It is a charge to have a Spiritual practice in life, to be connected, linked, with the Spirit in every way. Not "I did it my way," but "I did it the Spirit's way." Who are you listening to these days?

His divine power has given us everything needed for life and godliness, through the knowledge of him who called us by his own glory and goodness. Thus he has given us, through these things, his precious and very great promises, so that through them you may escape from the corruption that is in the world because of lust, and may become participants in the divine nature.

(2 Pet. 1:3–4)

Prayer for the Day

Spirit of the living God, fall afresh on me.

Day 7

Psalm 126; Isaiah 35:3–7; Luke 7:18–30

Glory, Glory, Hallelujah

Glory, glory, hallelujah!
Since I laid my burden down,
Glory, glory, hallelujah!
Since I laid my burden down.

I feel better, so much better!
Since I laid my burden down,
I feel better, so much better!
Since I laid my burden down.

Feel like shouting "Hallelujah!"
Since I laid my burden down,
Feel like shouting "Hallelujah!"
Since I laid my burden down.

I am climbing Jacob's ladder!
Since I laid my burden down,
I am climbing Jacob's ladder!
Since I laid my burden down.

Ev'ry round goes higher and higher!
Since I laid my burden down,
Ev'ry round goes higher and higher!
Since I laid my burden down.
                              —*Songs of Zion*, 98

Sometimes life is up. Sometimes life is down. There is joy and there is sorrow, and sometimes they are interwoven as a part of the human story, just as a crucifixion is interlocked with a resurrection. One cannot ignore present suffering on a hospital bed or the celebrations of birthdays or births. As Howard Thurman once said, "All around us worlds are dying and new worlds are being born" (*The Growing Edge*). There are burdens and there can be many, as it is repeated in the spiritual above, but the hope is that they have been laid down time after time. Burdens just don't go away; they continue to be a part of life as we continue to lay them down.

But intermixed with these burdens are also the outbursts of praise and joy. Glory, glory, hallelujah! I feel better! Feel like shouting! I am climbing! Going higher and higher! There is a reach to God, transcending the burdens, and this is the texture of life—the mingling of trouble and grace. Both are real, true, and unavoidable. Embrace the truth of life. Acknowledge that you have burdens that can be laid down. But confess praise to God that you are going higher on this day and your burdens will not bury you. Even if you don't feel like shouting, hopefully you feel better.

Strengthen the weak hands,
    and make firm the feeble knees.
Say to those who are of a fearful heart,
    "Be strong, do not fear!

Here is your God.
　He will come with vengeance,
with terrible recompense.
　He will come and save you."
Then the eyes of the blind shall be opened,
　and the ears of the deaf unstopped;
then the lame shall leap like a deer,
　and the tongue of the speechless sing for joy.
For waters shall break forth in the wilderness,
　and streams in the desert;
the burning sand shall become a pool,
　and the thirsty ground springs of water;
the haunt of jackals shall become a swamp,
　the grass shall become reeds and rushes.

(Isa. 35:3–7)

Prayer for the Day
Dear God, I want to lay my burdens down, not only to feel better but to be freed to sing, "Glory, Hallelujah!" Let it be so now.

Week Three

Day 1

Isaiah 12:2–6; Amos 6:1–8; 2 Corinthians 8:1–15

Certainly, Lord

Have you got good religion?	Cert'nly, Lord!
Have you got good religion?	Cert'nly, Lord!
Have you got good religion?	Cert'nly, Lord!
Cert'nly, Cert'nly, Cert'nly, Lord!	

Have you been redeemed?	Cert'nly, Lord!
Have you been redeemed?	Cert'nly, Lord!
Have you been redeemed?	Cert'nly, Lord!
Cert'nly, Cert'nly, Cert'nly, Lord!	

Have you been to the water?	Cert'nly Lord!
Have you been to the water?	Cert'nly Lord!
Have you been to the water?	Cert'nly Lord!
Cert'nly, Cert'nly, Cert'nly, Lord!	

Have you been baptized?	Cert'nly Lord!
Have you been baptized?	Cert'nly Lord!
Have you been baptized?	Cert'nly Lord!
Cert'nly, Cert'nly, Cert'nly, Lord!	

—*Songs of Zion*, 161

47

God asks us questions. We aren't the only ones inter-rogating God. The Psalms put questions in the mouth of humans: Why, Lord? How long? However, there are moments in the spiritual life when God may interrogate us to refocus us, to bring us back to the core. We can get caught up with the latest political issue or get lost in trivial matters of the day, but the divine questions come to us to shake us out of spiritual slumber: Have you got good religion? Have you been redeemed? Have you been to the water? Have you been baptized? "I know you've been running around doing a lot of good in the neighbor-hood, but have you got good religion?"

"Good religion" suggests there is bad religion. In the historical context of slavery, bad religion was a religion in the name of Christ that denigrated and dehumanized black people. Bad religion was professing one thing and doing another, a religion that endorsed second-class citi-zenship. Good religion was one that treated everybody as a child of God, treated everybody as a somebody. It walked the Christian talk. Underlying all of this is a par-ticular ethic, a way of life that is called for when one is redeemed and baptized.

It is a high ethical standard for a community—and notice that it is the community of faith that responds "Cert'nly Lord!" This song points to not only a "good religion" ethic but to the importance of community in the life of faith. We are not alone; we can be assured of faith by the pres-ence of others. We may falter in our answer to the ques-tions, but someone else can speak for us when we've lost our own voice. Even if we are uncertain, the community can sing out, "Cert'nly Lord!" The community can give us confidence and certainty and can help us work toward good religion. You might be redeemed, been to the water and been baptized, but do you have good religion?

Surely God is my salvation;
    I will trust, and will not be afraid,
for the Lord God is my strength and my might;
    he has become my salvation.
With joy you will draw water from the wells of
      salvation.
And you will say in that day:
Give thanks to the Lord,
    call on his name;
make known his deeds among the nations;
    proclaim that his name is exalted.
Sing praises to the Lord, for he has done gloriously;
    let this be known in all the earth.

(Isa. 12:2–5)

Prayer for the Day

Search me, O God, and perform an autopsy of my heart. Do I have good religion? If not, teach me this good way.

Day 2

Isaiah 12:2–6; Amos 8:4–12; 2 Corinthians 9:1–15

Oh, Rocks Don't Fall on Me

Oh, rocks don't fall on me,
Oh, rocks don't fall on me,
Oh, rocks don't fall on me,
Rocks and mountains don't fall on me.

Look over yonder on Jericho's walls,
Rocks and mountains don't fall on me,
See those sinners tremble and fall,
Rocks and mountains don't fall on me.

Oh, rocks don't fall on me,
Oh, rocks don't fall on me,
Oh, rocks don't fall on me,
Rocks and mountains don't fall on me.

In-a that great, great judg-a-ment day,
Rocks and mountains don't fall on me,
The sinner will run to the rocks and say,
Rocks and mountains please fall on me.

Oh, rocks please fall on me,
Oh, rocks please fall on me,
Oh, rocks please fall on me,
Rocks and mountains please fall on me.
    —*Folk Song of the American Negro* (1915), 58–59

A part of Advent is reflecting on the coming of God's judgment. God's coming isn't necessarily solely "joy to the world." It can also be "woe to the world." The promise of redemption also entails judgment. With judgment, the world, our world, as we know it, is torn apart, broken apart to be made whole. It is a new world order created by God's presence. Just as Jericho's walls came tumbling down, when God comes, worlds tumble and fall. The question is whether we will be left standing. Or, will the rocks and mountains fall on us, crushing us? In other words, are we ready for the coming of God? As the singer prays, "Oh, rocks don't fall on me," we ought to pray in preparation for what is to come. It is a repetitive plea. "Lord have mercy on me" is another way of saying, "Rocks don't fall on me." The next time you gaze at a mountain, as the ancients did Mount Zion, may it remind you of the coming of God and the need to pray constantly.

On that day, says the Lord GOD,
    I will make the sun go down at noon,
      and darken the earth in broad daylight.
I will turn your feasts into mourning,
      and all your songs into lamentation;
I will bring sackcloth on all loins,
      and baldness on every head;

I will make it like the mourning for an only son,
    and the end of it like a bitter day.
The time is surely coming, says the Lord God,
    when I will send a famine on the land;
not a famine of bread, or a thirst for water,
    but of hearing the words of the Lord.
They shall wander from sea to sea,
    and from north to east;
they shall run to and fro, seeking the word of the
        Lord,
    but they shall not find it.

                                        (Amos 8:9–12)

Prayer for the Day

Lord, have mercy on me, a sinner.

Day 3

Isaiah 12:2–6; Amos 9:8–15; Luke 1:57–66

Live a-Humble

Refrain
Live a-humble, humble,
Humble yourself,
The bells done rung.
Live a-humble, humble,
Humble yourself,
The bells done rung.

You see God, you see God,
You see God 'n the morning,
He'll come a-riding down the line of time,
Fire'll be falling, He'll be calling,
Come to judg-a-ment-a-come.
Refrain

Oh, the bells done rung,
And the songs done sung,
And-a don't let it catch you with your work undone.
Refrain
　　　　—*Folk Song of the American Negro* (1915), 74

The bells are ringing and people are singing. Fire is fall-ing. God is riding and calling. Images of judgment day in the morning of our future. These images reach to com-prehend the experience of seeing God in the morning "a-riding down the line of time." There isn't necessar-ily fear, though fire falling could ignite that in a heart. But there is insight into how to live in the light of God's coming.

Amid the bells, songs, and the cacophony of worldly sounds, how do you conduct your life? What is your posture, even in a society that emphasizes getting ahead of everyone else or climbing up the ladder of success? The lesson given is to "live a-humble." "Humble your-self." This is about you, not a family member or a friend. Humble. Close to the ground, from the earth, *humus*. This way was taken by God in Christ when he emptied, humbled himself (Philippians 2). This way of living is not popular—and it may kill you doing it—but it dem-onstrates the recognition that you are not God. It shows that you understand your place in the world in the face of the coming God.

God is the main act. We are warm-up acts to the grand theater of God's handiwork in the world. If you "see God," you'll have no choice but to see yourself for who you are, a humble child of God. Get close to the ground again and find your true self.

> The time is surely coming, says the Lord,
>> when the one who plows shall overtake the one
>>> who reaps,
>> and the treader of grapes the one who sows the
>>> seed;
> the mountains shall drip sweet wine,
>> and all the hills shall flow with it.

I will restore the fortunes of my people Israel,
   and they shall rebuild the ruined cities and inhabit
      them;
they shall plant vineyards and drink their wine,
   and they shall make gardens and eat their fruit.
I will plant them upon their land,
   and they shall never again be plucked up
   out of the land that I have given them,
says the Lord your God.

(Amos 9:13–15)

Prayer for the Day

God, allow my heart to be so humble as to be a portal for your presence. Ride on and let me humbly follow.

Day 4

Isaiah 12:2–6; Zephaniah 3:14–20;
Luke 3:7–18; Philippians 4:4–7

Good News, the Chariot's Coming

Refrain
Good news, the chariot's coming,
Good news, the chariot's coming,
Good news, the chariot's coming,
And I don't want-her to leave-a-me behind.

It's a golden chariot,—Carry me home,
A golden chariot,—Carry me home,
A golden chariot,—Carry me home,
And I don't want-her to leave-a-me behind.
Refrain

There's a long white robe, In the heaven I know;
A long white robe,—In the heaven I know;
A long white robe,—In the heaven I know;
And I don't want-her to leave-a-me behind.
Refrain
          —*Folk Song of the American Negro* (1915), 49

The Advent season with its inclusion of judgment at the coming of God can bring a sense of fear. But the promise of God's advent also brings hope and is good news. It is good news that "the chariot's coming." The chariot or other images, such as trains, in the spirituals are the vehicles that signal travel home, to God's world, heaven. Part of the good news is that the chariot is coming because it doesn't have to come, just like God is not forced to come. Of course, we don't want to be left behind, because who wouldn't want to go home?

Home is with God, a resting place. That there is an ultimate home should bring some comfort. That we must travel or move with the chariot suggests that we are pilgrims passing through this barren land. We are a people on the move. But where are you going? What is your ultimate hope? The good news is that God is willing to come and is coming. We don't know when nor do we really know how. But we know God is coming. That alone is good news and a source of joy.

> Sing aloud, O daughter Zion;
>   shout, O Israel!
> Rejoice and exult with all your heart,
>   O daughter Jerusalem!
> The LORD has taken away the judgments against you,
>   he has turned away your enemies.
> The king of Israel, the LORD, is in your midst;
>   you shall fear disaster no more.

(Zeph. 3:14–15)

Prayer for the Day

Advent God, fill my heart in knowing that you love me so much that you are coming. Let that good news be on my lips this day.

Day 5

Numbers 16:1–19; Isaiah 11:1–9; Hebrews 13:7–17

Climbin' Up d' Mountain

Refrain
Climbin' up d'mountain, children (Good Lawd, Ah).
Didn't come here for to stay (Oh, my Lawd, and),
If ah nevermore see you again, gonna meet you at de
    judgment day.
(Hallelujah, Lawd, Ah'm [repeat])

Hebrew children in de fiery furnace (Oh Lawd).
And dey begin to pray (Oh Lawd),
And de good Lawd smote dat fire out.
(Oh, wasn't dat a mighty day! Good Lawd, wasn't dat a
    mighty day!)
Dat's why Ah'm
Refrain

Daniel went in de lion's den (Oh, Lawd),
And he begin to pray (Oh, Lawd),
And de angel of de Lawd locked de lion's jaw.

(Oh, wasn't dat a mighty day! Good Lawd, wasn't dat a
   mighty day!)
Dat's why Ah'm
Refrain

—Songs of Zion, 120

Whether it be the three Hebrew children—Shadrach,
Meshach, and Abednego—in the fiery furnace or Daniel
in the lion's den, there is a clear message of God's intervention. Those biblical stories point to the future freedom that awaits the children of God. I "didn't come here
for to stay" means that the situation we find ourselves in
at this moment in history is not eternal. We might have
to climb mountains, sit in furnaces, and fight off lions, but
none of these will prevent the presence of God.

We climb mountains knowing that one day we will be
moving to even higher ground and it will be "a mighty
day!" We will join Daniel and the Hebrew children and
other saints of old to testify that we too have been delivered and embrace the judgment day with hope to such
an extent that we can sing "hallelujah, Lawd." Climb the
mountain even if it is in a furnace because God is there
reminding you that you won't be there, wherever it is,
forever. Get ready for moving day!

> The wolf shall live with the lamb,
>   the leopard shall lie down with the kid,
> the calf and the lion and the fatling together,
>   and a little child shall lead them.
> The cow and the bear shall graze,
>   their young shall lie down together;
>   and the lion shall eat straw like the ox.

The nursing child shall play over the hole of the asp,
    and the weaned child shall put its hand on the
        adder's den.
They will not hurt or destroy
    on all my holy mountain;
for the earth will be full of the knowledge of the
    Lord
    as the waters cover the sea.

(Isa. 11:6–9)

Prayer for the Day

Remind me, O God, that I didn't come here to stay but am on my way to You. Hallelujah, Lord!

Day 6

Numbers 16:20–35; Isaiah 11:1–9; Acts 28:23–31

The Day of Judgment

And de moon will turn to blood,
And de moon will turn to blood,
And de moon will turn to blood
In dat day—O—yoy,* my soul!
And de moon will turn to blood in dat day.

2. And you'll see de stars a-fallin' . . .

3. And de world will be on fire . . .

4. And you'll hear de saints a-singin' . . .

5. And de Lord will say to de sheep . . .

6. For to go to Him right hand . . .

7. But de goats must go to de left . . .
—*Slave Songs of the United States*
(1867), 72

* "A sort of prolonged wail."

61

This Advent season provides a liturgical time for reflection on one's life in light of the coming of God. God is love but God is also a loving judge, loving justice. Throughout Scripture, we hear about being "set apart," which is where we get the word "sanctification." To "sanctify" is to make holy. We don't normally talk about personal or social holiness much. If we do mention holiness, it is usually focused on the holiness of God. Yet we hear throughout Scripture, "be holy, for I am holy" (see Lev. 11:45b; 1 Pet. 1:16). Be set apart. At the coming of God, on judgment day, when the world turns, and the moon turns to blood, when the stars fall, and the saints sing, "de Lord" will say to "de sheep," hopefully us, go to the right, which is to him, and the goats to the left. We probably don't think about this daily, but this season nudges us to reflect on this.

Are you a sheep or a goat? Will you go to him or away from him? The world will be on fire but the saints will keep singing and not get burned. What will you do on that day? I hope you sing or at least say, "Baa baa."

> Then the LORD spoke to Moses and to Aaron, saying: Separate yourselves from this congregation, so that I may consume them in a moment. They fell on their faces, and said, "O God, the God of the spirits of all flesh, shall one person sin and you become angry with the whole congregation?"
>
> (Num. 16:20–22)

Prayer for the Day
When the world is going crazy, allow me to remain sane and sing with all the saints.

Day 7

Isaiah 11:1–9; Micah 4:8–13; Luke 7:31–35

Somebody's Knocking at Your Door

Somebody's knocking at your door,
Somebody's knocking at your door,
O . . . sinner, why don't you answer?
Somebody's knocking at your door.

Knocks like Jesus,
Somebody's knocking at your door.
Knocks like Jesus,
Somebody's knocking at your door.
O . . . sinner, why don't you answer?
Somebody's knocking at your door.

Can't you hear him?
Somebody's knocking at your door.
Can't you hear him?
Somebody's knocking at your door.
O . . . sinner, why don't you answer?
Somebody's knocking at your door.

Answer Jesus,
Somebody's knocking at your door.
Answer Jesus,
Somebody's knocking at your door.
O . . . sinner, why don't you answer?
Somebody's knocking at your door.

Can't you trust him?
Somebody's knocking at your door.
Can't you trust him?
Somebody's knocking at your door.
O . . . sinner, why don't you answer?
Somebody's knocking at your door.
—*American Negro Songs* (1940), 192*

In the context of fear and not knowing if or when you would be stolen away to death at the hands of hate-filled people, an enslaved person, even if he had his own living quarters, might be leery of opening the door when someone knocked because he didn't know what was on the other side. It might indeed have been Death knocking, so there was a lot of suspicion, not surprisingly. This spiritual, however, takes up this knocking-at-the-door image from Scripture—"Behold I stand at the door and knock" (Revelation 3:20)—and links it to Jesus.

Repeatedly, we hear, "Somebody's knocking at your door." The questions are: Why don't you answer? Can't you hear him? Can't you trust him? First, it is clear that the initiative comes from Jesus. He knocks. He comes. He loves first. He loves always and that love is always knocking at the door of our hearts. Second, however, is

* John Wesley Work (ed.), *American Negro Songs* (New York: Howell, Soskin & Co., 1940).

whether we hear him, or if the clamoring of life blocks the sound of the knock. Third, even if we hear the knocking, do we trust enough to open the door to Jesus? We can hear but never trust, never take the risk to answer and then follow. Perhaps we don't know what to expect from him, so we don't answer. If we don't answer, it will be our loss because we will miss out on an inextinguishable love. But you know what? Even if we don't hear, or trust, or answer, he continues to knock. He continues to be present. He never leaves nor forsakes us. The next time you play the "knock knock" game, remember this: "Knock, knock." "Who's there?" Jesus.

> "To what then will I compare the people of this generation, and what are they like? They are like children sitting in the marketplace and calling to one another, 'We played the flute for you, and you did not dance; we wailed, and you did not weep.' For John the Baptist has come eating no bread and drinking no wine, and you say, 'He has a demon'; the Son of Man has come eating and drinking, and you say, 'Look, a glutton and a drunkard, a friend of tax collectors and sinners!' Nevertheless, wisdom is vindicated by all her children."
>
> (Luke 7:31–35)

Prayer for the Day
As you knock at the door of my life, give me courage to answer and open the door to eternal life and love.

Week Four

Day 1

Psalm 80:1–7; Jeremiah 31:31–34; Hebrews 10:10–18

Done Foun' My Los' Sheep

Refrain
Done foun' my los' sheep,
Done foun' my los' sheep,
Done foun' my los' sheep, Hallelujah.

I done foun' my los' sheep,
Done foun' my los' sheep,
Done foun' my los' sheep.

My Lord had one hundred sheep,
One o' dem did go astray,
That jes lef' Him nine-ty-nine,
Go to de wilderness, seek an' fin',
Ef you fin' him, bring him back,
Cross de shoulders,
Cross yo' back;
Tell de neighbors all aroun',
Dat los' sheep has done be foun'
Refrain

In dat Resurrection Day sinner can't fin no hidin' place,
Go to de mountain, de mountain move;
Run to de hill, de hill run too.
Sinner man trablin' on trembling groun';
Po' los' sheep aint nebber been foun'
Sinner why don't yo' stop and pray,
Den you'd hear de Shepherd say,
Refrain

— *The Books of American Negro Spirituals*,
vol. 1 (1925), 167–69[*]

Not everyone who is lost wants to be found, even when
they've lost who they are at their core. They are the "los'
sheep," the ones who "aint nebber been foun'." Maybe
this is you or someone you know. "Why don't yo' stop
and pray?" Pray for yourself. Pray for the person you
know is lost. To pray is a way of stopping the direction
one is heading. To pray is to suggest that there is One
who can find us. In fact, there is one who seeks us out
even if we are in a wilderness. "Seek an' fin', / Ef you fin'
him, bring him back." If we stop and slow down, we may
not only discover that we are lost but that there is one
desiring to find us to bring us back into the fold. God's
love lures him to us and God is adamant about saying,
"done foun' my los' sheep." This is what God wants to
testify. If you are lost, God wants to find you today.

Restore us, O God; let your face shine, that we may
be saved.

(Ps. 80:3)

[*] James Weldon Johnson and J. Rosamond Johnson, eds., *The Books of American Negro Spirituals*, vol. 1 (New York: Viking Press, 1925).

Prayer for the Day

Seeking God, please find me. I am lost and need to be found again.

Day 2

Psalm 80:1–7; Isaiah 42:10–18; Hebrews 10:32–39

Mah God Is So High

Refrain
Mah God is so high, yuh can't get over Him;
He's so low, yuh can't git under Him;
He's so wide, yuh can't get aroun' Him;
Yuh mus' come in by an through de Lam'.

One day as I was a-walkin' along de Hebenly road,
Mah Savior spoke unto me an' He fill mah heart wid
   His love.
Refrain

I'll take mah gospel trumpet an' I'll begin to blow,
An' if mah Savior help me I'll blow wherever I go.
Refrain

—*Songs of Zion*, 105

How big is your God? Does God fit into your thinking
and tradition and your desires? Or is God larger than

you can even imagine? It's so easy to slot God into our political, theological, and economic camps, making God into our limited image with our limited understanding, and thus limiting God. But God and God's resources are limitless. This is the God who comes.

This spiritual paints that portrait beautifully. God is so high you can't get over him, so low you can't get under him, so wide you can't get around him. Basically, you can't "get one over" on God. You can't figure God out in God's totality. God is too big for us to fully comprehend. If we got over God, we might think that we were God. This spiritual helps us affirm the expansiveness of God and yet understand how God allows us to come to know God "through de Lam'." God is universal and particular. God is transcendent and immanent. So even though God is high and wide, God wants us to know him in Jesus, the Savior.

This path of knowing God should spark some joy on the road of life, to know that there is such a big God for little humanity. God is not so big that God forgot the world. God so loved the world that he gave his Son (John 3:16). This doesn't mean that God fits into your box. It just means that God's love is vast and God offers the gift of Christ to us. Let that news cause you to pick up your gospel trumpet and blow wherever you go!

> Sing to the LORD a new song,
>   his praise from the end of the earth!
> Let the sea roar and all that fills it,
>   the coastlands and their inhabitants.
> Let the desert and its towns lift up their voice,
>   the villages that Kedar inhabits;
> let the inhabitants of Sela sing for joy,
>   let them shout from the tops of the mountains.

> Let them give glory to the LORD,
>   and declare his praise in the coastlands.
>   (Isa. 42:10–12)

Prayer for the Day

God, you are not so big or so far away that you refuse to come near to me. Come close that I may sing and know your love.

Day 3

Psalm 80:1–7; Isaiah 66:7–11; Luke 13:31–35

Freedom Train a-Comin'

Hear that-a freedom train a-coming, coming, coming,
Hear that freedom train a-coming, coming, coming,
Hear that freedom train a-coming, coming, coming,
Get on board, oh, oh, get on board.

It'll be carryin' nothing but freedom, freedom, freedom, . . .
Get on board, get on board.

They'll be comin' by the thousand, thousand, thousand, . . .
Get on board, get on board.

It'll be carryin' freedom fighters, fighters, fighters, . . .
Get on board, get on board.

It'll be carryin' registered voters, voters, voters, . . .
Get on board, get on board.

It'll be rollin' through Mississippi, Mississippi, Mississippi, . . .
Get on board, get on board.

—*Songs of Zion*, 92

The image of a train in the Spirituals is prominent. Sometimes it can refer to a life-giving situation. Other times, it is a train transporting one to death. In this case, this train brings freedom. This is heavenly and earthly freedom. There's a double meaning, which is prevalent in many Spirituals. There is a text and sub-text. The freedom train could be about going to heaven, encouraging passengers to "get on board." But this train also has earthly significance, which must not be ignored.

Historically, the freedom train traveled north to Canada, away from the chains of slavery. The enslaved used songs as code to send messages. What you see above in the lyrics is also the fluidity of lyrics, that is, how they can change based on certain contextual circumstances. The talk about "registered voters" or "rollin' through Mississippi" is linked to the struggle for civil rights in the 1960s, but even this example embodies how freedom is both transcendent and immanent. The two understandings are connected and shouldn't be separated. If they were, then one might be charged with being heavenly-minded and no earthly-good or so earthly-minded that one isn't heavenly-good.

The challenge and opportunity are to think about freedom, even your freedom, in a broader way. When Christ came to set us free and to save us, the freedom involved is much wider than sometimes presented. Christ came to bring salvation, which is wholeness, and this includes our entire life, the inner life and outer life, inner freedom and outer freedom. With this in mind, ask yourself, "Am I free?" If not, the freedom train's a-coming, and I hope you get on board before it's too late.

Before she was in labor
   she gave birth;
before her pain came upon her
   she delivered a son.
Who has heard of such a thing?
   Who has seen such things?
Shall a land be born in one day?
   Shall a nation be delivered in one moment?
Yet as soon as Zion was in labor
   she delivered her children.
Shall I open the womb and not deliver?
   says the LORD;
shall I, the one who delivers, shut the womb?
   says your God.

(Isa. 66:7–9)

Prayer for the Day
God, I want to be free.

Day 4

Micah 5:2–5a; Luke 1:46b–55 or Psalm 80:1–7;
Luke 1:39–45 [46–55]; Hebrews 10:5–10

Balm in Gilead

Refrain
There is a balm in Gilead, to make the wounded whole,
There is a balm in Gilead, to heal the sin-sick soul,

Sometimes I feel discouraged,
And think my work's in vain,
But then the Holy Spirit
Revives my soul again.
Refrain

Don't ever feel discouraged,
For Jesus is your friend,
And if you look for knowledge,
He'll ne'er refuse to lend.
Refrain

If you cannot preach like Peter,
If you cannot pray like Paul,

you can tell the love of Jesus,
And say "He died for all."
Refrain
—*Songs of Zion*, 123

This spiritual is the epitome of hope, but it isn't a hope that is disconnected from the reality of life. The refrain rings out, "There is a balm in Gilead." It is courageous. It is bold. It is faith-filled. It turns the prophet Jeremiah's question, "Is there no balm in Gilead?" into an exclamation point—there is a balm! In the life of faith, there are days when this may be our song, full of assurance. Yet there are other days when we may be unsure about everything, including God.

Sometimes you may feel discouraged and think your work's in vain. Other times, you may lack knowledge and recognize your limitations in that you can't preach like Peter or pray like Paul. There are days when you are down and life isn't a bunch of sweet-smelling red roses. That's what this spiritual acknowledges. But each time you are down, the verse also makes a turn and points up: "but then the Holy Spirit revives my soul again"; "He'll ne'er refuse to lend"; "you can tell the love of Jesus." These verses embody the human reality of ups and downs and provide, in the midst of these realities, hope. In fact, hope would not be hope if it didn't arise amid our struggles. Hope rises from the ashes and earthquake rubble. It wouldn't be hope if it was anything different. Got hope? Do you believe there is a balm in Gilead to heal and make you whole? The Advent season proclaims there is a balm. If there wasn't, God would have never come to earth.

And Mary said,
"My soul magnifies the Lord,
    and my spirit rejoices in God my Savior,
for he has looked with favor on the lowliness of
        his servant."

(Luke 1:46–48a)

Prayer for the Day

Balm in Gilead, spread your healing across this wounded world
so hope can be born again in our hearts.

Day 5

Genesis 25:19–28; Psalm 113; Colossians 1:15–20

I Hear from Heaven To-day

Hurry on, my weary soul,
And I yearde from heaven to-day,
Hurry on, my weary soul,
And I yearde from heaven to-day

My sin is forgiven and my soul set free,
And I yearde from heaven to-day,
My sin is forgiven and my soul set free,
And I yearde from heaven to-day.

A baby born in Bethlehem,
And I yearde from heaven to-day.
A baby born in Bethlehem,
And I yearde from heaven to-day.

De trumpet sound in de oder bright land,
And I yearde from heaven to-day.
De trumpet sound in de oder bright land,
And I yearde from heaven to-day.

> My name is called and I must go,
> And I yearde from heaven to-day.
> My name is called and I must go,
> And I yearde from heaven to-day.
>
> De bell is a-ringin' in de oder bright world.
> And I yearde from heaven to-day.
> De bell is a-ringin' in de oder bright world.
> And I yearde from heaven to-day.
> —*Slave Songs of the United States* (1867), 3

We often pray, "on earth as it is in heaven." But there will come a time when the earth, as we know it, will be no more. As promised, there will be a "new heaven and a new earth." In the meantime, there are glimpses of the heavenly glory on earth. There are reminders that there is a world beyond this one. There is a Voice that is not our own voice, so as one speaks of hearing from heaven today, it points to the experience of God on earth. It points to hearing good news today, not tomorrow or yesterday. It affirms that "today is the day of salvation" (2 Corinthians 6:2). You can experience the gifts of God right now.

When one is weary, the gift of God's presence can spur one to "hurry on." It can also affirm forgiveness and freedom in the here and now. The pronouncement of the birth of Jesus comes in heavenly breaking news as well. The trumpet will eventually sound, signifying the coming of a new day and new world. There will come a time when we all will declare, "I must go," because we "yearde from heaven." There is a time for everything under heaven and there will be a time when time will be no more. Trumpets and bells will signify a new order and world of God. It'll be bright. It'll be sunny because there will be the eternal light of Christ. Do we have eyes to see and ears to hear from heaven today, or is this sound blocked out from other distracting noises?

> Praise the LORD!
> Praise, O servants of the LORD;
>   praise the name of the LORD.
> Blessed be the name of the LORD
>   from this time on and forevermore.
> From the rising of the sun to its setting
>   the name of the LORD is to be praised.
> The LORD is high above all nations,
>   and his glory above the heavens.
>   (Ps. 113:1–4)

Prayer for the Day

Dear God, open my ears to hear from heaven today.

Day 6

Genesis 30:1–24; Psalm 113; Romans 8:18–30

Study War No More

I'm a-going to lay down my sword and shield
Down by the riverside,
Down by the riverside,
Down by the riverside,
Going to lay down my sword and shield,
Down by the riverside,
Ain't going to study war no more.

Refrain
Ain't going to study war no more,
Ain't going to study war no more,
Ain't going to study war no more,
Ain't going to study war no more,
Ain't going to study war no more,
Ain't going to study war no more.

I'm a-going to put on my long white robe
Down by the riverside, down by the riverside, down by
the riverside.
I'm a-going to put on my long white robe

Down by the riverside.
Ain't going to study war no more.
Refrain

I'm a-going to talk with the Prince of Peace
Down by the riverside, down by the riverside, down by
the riverside.
I'm a-going to talk with the Prince of Peace
Down by the riverside.
Ain't going to study war no more.
Refrain

—*American Negro Songs* (1940), 202–3

The world is full of trials, tribulations, and tensions. Fighting seems to be at a feverish pitch, drowning out even the faintest sound of peace or hope. War doesn't solely have to be between nations or political parties. War may happen in families or other relationships. War might be winning inside of you, as you grapple with personal struggles. Because of the ongoing battles, external or internal, you may always be ready for a good fight, but there are no winners in a fight. Your sword and shield are at your right hand and you are always on guard, in defensive mode. There seems to be no rest.

In contrast, at the riverside of God's kingdom there are cool, calm waters of peace, stirred by the Prince of Peace. There will be a day, as the Scriptures tell us, when swords will become plowshares, and we will lay down our sword and shield. But let this image of future action become present for you. Drink from the wells of God's river as God leads you beside the still waters. You can go down by the riverside today in the Spirit to experience nonviolence and peace in your soul. You don't have to wait to talk with the Prince of Peace. Let him whisper joy and wisdom in your ear today. Put down your armor or your guard and give yourself over to the refreshing rivers of God's hope. No more fighting. No more battles. Let peace like a river fill your soul. Wade in the water.

> For in hope we were saved. Now hope that is seen is not hope. For who hopes for what is seen? But if we hope for what we do not see, we wait for it with patience.
>
> (Rom. 8:24–25)

Prayer for the Day
Creator God, you formed the waters of the world, so lead me to the riverside to drink from your everlasting peace that all warring may cease, even in my life.

Day 7

Psalm 96; Isaiah 9:2–7;
Luke 2:1–14 [15–20]; Titus 2:11–14

Rise Up, Shepherd, and Follow

There's a star in the east on Christmas morn.
Rise up, shepherd, and follow.
It will lead to the place where the Christ was born.
Rise up, shepherd, and follow.

Refrain
Follow, follow;
Rise up, shepherd, and follow.
Follow the star of Bethlehem.
Rise up, shepherd, and follow.

If you take good heed to the angel's words,
Rise up, shepherd, and follow.
You'll forget your flocks, you'll forget your herds.
Rise up, shepherd, and follow.
Refrain

—*The Books of American Negro Spirituals*,
vol. 2, 66–67[*]

---

[*] James Weldon Johnson and J. Rosamond Johnson, eds., *The Books of American Negro Spirituals*, vol. 2 (New York: Viking Press, 1926).

God brings love into the world through Jesus Christ, the babe born in Bethlehem. When Jesus is born, there are visual and aural/oral signs. There's a star in the east and an angel speaks. These happen as a response to Christ's birth but it is not enough for his birth to touch the heavens via stars and angels. Christ's birth touches the earth as well. It touches you. This is where the shepherds come in. This is where you come in. If Christ was born and nothing ever changed on earth, what would the point be of his coming? Clearly, something happens on earth and thus the shepherds respond.

They do two things: rise up and follow. One can rise and remain stagnant, but the shepherds follow. They may not know exactly where he's going but follow the cosmic sign of the star to eventually see the Light, the Bright and Morning Star, of the world. The shepherds can't help but follow, because God's presence on earth has lifted them, resurrected them, and caused them to rise up. They might have been breathing but weren't fully alive, weren't fully up, without Jesus. Now they're resurrected through the baby who is the resurrection and the life. They can rise up and follow wherever Christ leads.

Perhaps you need to rise up and recognize the life of God in a little baby in Bethlehem. You've been taking care of your flocks and herds daily but for whatever reason you feel down and there's no movement in your life, nothing worthwhile to follow. Yet Christ will raise you up and get you moving, if you see and hear the signs around you. This is what incarnate love does. It lifts you and propels you forward. You may be down but ask God to help you to rise up today.

In that region there were shepherds living in the fields, keeping watch over their flock by night. Then an angel of the Lord stood before them, and the glory of the Lord shone around them, and they were terrified. But the angel said to them, "Do not be afraid; for see—I am bringing you good news of great joy for all the people."

(Luke 2:8–10)

Prayer for the Day

Guiding Lord, help me to follow you wherever you lead. Open my eyes to see the signposts of your glory. Let me rise up and follow.